I0138119

SEPHARIAL'S
ARCANA & KEYS

THE ARCANA OR STOCK & SHARE KEY

THE KEY TO SUGAR VALUES

THE KEY TO RUBBER

THE MASTER KEY

THE GOLDEN KEY

THE ECLIPSE SYSTEM

THE SOLAR LUNAR VALUES

THE SOLAR APEX METHOD

BY

SEPHARIAL

(WALTER GORN OLD)

COSMOLOGICAL ECONOMICS
WWW.COSMOECONOMICS.COM

ORIGINALLY PUBLISHED 1920-1930

THIS EDITION © COPYRIGHT 2015
COSMOLOGICAL ECONOMICS
WWW.COSMOECONOMICS.COM

THIS SERIES IS PUBLISHED BY THE:
INSTITUTE OF COSMOLOGICAL ECONOMICS

COSMOLOGICAL ECONOMICS
IS AN IMPRINT OF:
SACRED SCIENCE INSTITUTE
WWW.SACREDSCIENCE.COM
INSTITUTE@SACREDSCIENCE.COM
US: 800-756-6141 θ INTL: 951-659-8181

COSMOLOGICAL ECONOMICS

THE MASTERS OF FINANCIAL ASTROLOGY SERIES

The Masters of Financial Astrology Series brings together a collection of the most important classical and modern works on Astroeconomics or astrological financial market forecasting. These classic works written from the Golden Age of Technical Analysis to current times were carefully selected by the late Dr. Jerome Baumring of the Investment Centre Bookstore in the 1980's, as representing the most valuable and important works in financial astrology ever written. They were included as the foundational source texts for his program in advanced financial market analysis and forecasting, and serve as the ideal foundation for any analyst seeking a thorough education in astrological applications to financial market theory and forecasting.

The Golden Age of technical analysis was a period from the early 1900's through the 1960's where the foundational theories of modern financial analysis and financial astrology came into full form. The ideas and technologies developed during this fruitful period include the first serious research into the modern field of Astro-Economics, or Financial Astrology and related fields like cycle analysis, cosmic causation, solar influence on geomagnetic and Earthly events like weather, earthquakes, climate change and radio disturbance. Though financial astrology is actually a subject that stretches back centuries, if not millennia, this ripe period saw the real advent of popular research and theoretical development of this vast study of the interaction between cosmic forces and Earthly phenomena. This collection represents the best work available within this field.

Each quality reprint of these classical texts has been reproduced as an exact facsimile of the original text, maintaining the original layout, typeset, charts, and style of the author and time period, helping to preserve and communicate a sense of the feeling of the original work that a reproduction in modern format does not capture.

Many of these rare works and courses were originally printed in only very small private editions or as correspondence courses, so that the originals were easily lost or destroyed over time. Our reproductions of these important source works are printed on acid free paper and bound in a quality hardcover that will compliment any trading library and help to preserve this important resource for generations to come.

The series is also currently being digitized and archived for permanent digital preservation by the Institute of Cosmological Economics, creating a searchable reference library of market wisdom accessible globally and available in new digital formats to keep the knowledge fresh and accessible through new devices and technology as we advance further into the information revolution. To see our full catalog of hardcover reprints, new publications, and digital editions please visit our website at www.CosmoEconomics.com.

Sepharial's Arcana & Keys

Publisher's Introduction

Sepharial, whose actual name was Walter Gorn Old, was born in 1864 in Birmingham England, and died in 1929 having gained the reputation of being one of the best astrologers of the foundational age of the modern astrological tradition. Old was a child prodigy who began studying astrology when he was only 15 and who wrote his first of over 30 books when he was just 23 years old. He was a close friend of Helena Blavatsky and a member of the inner circle of the Theosophical Society, so was well positioned in the center of the occult and esoteric world of the late 19th and early 20th century.

His Arcanas or Keys are his rarest and most secretive writings, being distilled applications of his most important techniques and systems, offered exclusively to his most private clients. To acquire these writings Sepharial required a written application and signature of a non-disclosure agreement. Due to these restrictions, these writings have always been the most difficult of Sepharial work to find, and only a small number of them have even survived. This set represents the most complete collection known of these rarest of Sepharial's writings.

The Arcana of Stock & Share Key, Key to Sugar Values, and Rubber are exact facsimiles of the original documents. The Master Key, Golden Key & Eclipse System are transcribed reproductions, of these very rare works primarily focused on forecasting of horse races.

About the Master Key, Sepharial said, *"This system is deemed to be the final word in racing Systems. It embodies the result of 11 years of observation and research and is itself the easiest and most reliable of the many attempts that have been made to fathom the profundities of racing problems and it is claimed that The Master Key leaves others behind and gives the best results."*

The Golden Key, Sepharial comments, *"is only published in typed script under an agreement which secures privacy and non-publication. This is the method I have employed in regard to all my Arcana. It would have been quite easy for me to have published the Golden Key as a book and in all probability it would have sold in thousands at a good price. But in doing so I should have emasculated its working value to all who possessed it."*

The Eclipse System was written sometime after the Golden Key, to which it refers, and it mentions recent racing from 1917. Some consider this Sepharial's most reliable system. The Solar Lunar Values & Solar Apex Method are brief summaries of the rules applied by these systems. Altogether this is the most complete collection of these rare materials ever offered, and should serve as an excellent guide into Sepharials deepest work.

William Bradstreet Stewart, Director
Institute of Cosmological Economics

TABLE OF CONTENTS

∞

THE ARCANA OR STOCK & SHARE KEY

BY

SEPHARIAL

LONDON STOCK EXCHANGE HOROSCOPE

May 18th 1801 @ 12 Noon: London, Eng.

S.T. Gr-noon 3-42-45
S.T. at birth 3-42-57

G.M.T. 12 Noon

Adj. Calc. Date: May 18th 1801

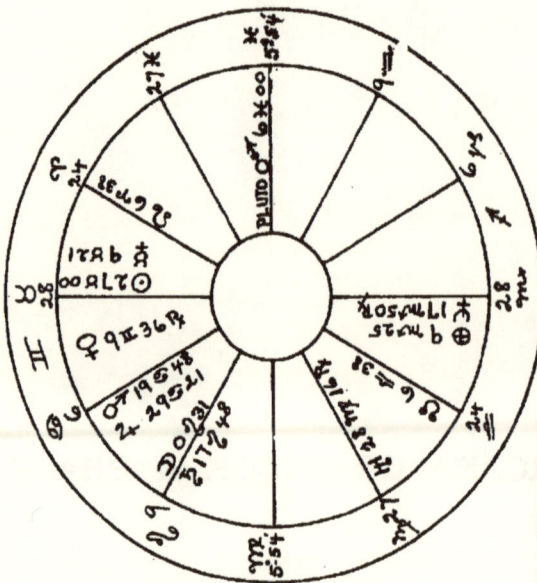

Declinations
⊙ 19-31 n
☽ 24-41 n
☿ 12-45 n
♀ 25-04 n
♂ 23-29 n
♃ 20-55 n
♄ 16-46 n
♅ 1-23 n
♆ 15-31 s

NEW YORK STOCK EXCHANGE HOROSCOPE

May 17th 1792 @ 12 Noon: New York city

S.T. Gr-noon 3-43-11
S.T. at birth 3-42-57

G.M.T. 5 P.M.

Adj. Calc. Date: March 2nd 1792

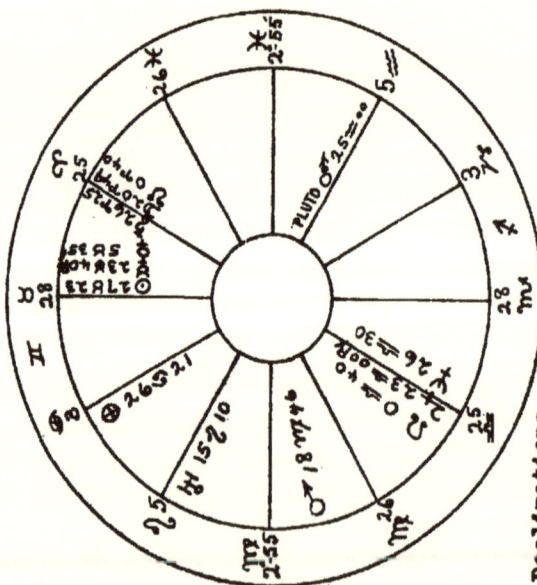

Declinations
⊙ 19-36 n
☽ 6-45 n
☿ 18-05 n
♀ 18-00 n
♂ 6-18 n
♃ 7-36 s
♄ 8-02 n
♅ 16-57 n
♆ 9-00 s

THE ARCANA or STOCK AND SHARE KEY BY   SEPHARIAL

_____

The RADIX of any company is the noon of the date and

place of registration of that Company, whereby, under

the laws of the country the promotors are given powers

to form the company and proceed with business.

The RADIX of a Stock Exchange IS THE NOON OF THE DATE

OF FOUNDING. The charts for New York and London are

attached hereto and will serve as examples of all others,

FROM THIS RADIX or root figure of the heavens a variety

of influences are by natural process of celestrial mo-

tions indicated. These are found to depend altogether

upon the Sun, which is the controlling center of their

interactions. The Sun's MAN MOTION IS 59 minutes and

eight seconds per day. The measure of TIME IS ONE DAY

FOR A YEAR. Thus the influences arising out of the move-

ment of the bodies in relation to the Sun will influence

successive years of the Company, the indications arising

in the second day affecting the second year, those form-

ed on the third day influence the third year, and so on

continuously.

SOLAR MOTION: THE APPARENT MOTION OF THE SUN AS SEEN

FROM THE EARTH is slightly variable, according to the

season of the year. This is due to the fact that the

apparent orbit of the Sun is not concentric with the

earth but is slightly removed therefrom, thus producing
an eccentricity of its apparent motion about the earth,
and this may amount to as much as one degree and fifty
six minutes either way, as compared with its mean, or
average motion, which is 59 minutes 8 seconds per day. It
has been found in a great number of tests that the MEAN MO-
TION OF THE SUN IS THE CORRECT MEASURE TO BE OBSERVED, AND
THE SUN REQUIRES 365 1/4 days to complete the circle of
360 degrees we have a mean motion of 59 minutes 8 seconds
per day.

This amount is multiplied by the number of years from
the radix or date of registration and added to the Sun's
place in the radix (called Sun r), also to the Midheaven,
and to the Moon r. The other planets are in the same way
carried forward through the zodiac at the same rate as the
Sun and maintain their radical relations with the Sun there-
by, but in the course of their progress from day to day at
this uniform rate, they form aspects to the radical places
of the Sun, Midheaven, Moon, and ascendant of the radix.
These aspects are called DIRECTIONAL ASPECTS and they IN-
FLUENCE THE AFFAIRS OF THE COMPANY OR THE BUSINESS OF ANY
EXCHANGE ACCORDING TO THEIR SEVERAL NATURES.

THE PRIME SIGNIFICATOR OF ANY CHART IS THAT PLANET
WHICH RULES THE SIGN IN WHICH THE SUN IS FOUND. Thus,
in the chart for the New York Stock Exchange, the Sun
is in the sign Taurus. This sign is ruled by Venus, and
Venus therefore becomes PRIME SIGNIFICATOR.

THE SECONDARY SIGNIFICATOR IS THE PLANET WHICH RULES
THE DECANATE IN WHICH THE PRIME SIGNIFICATOR HAPPENS TO BE
PASSING THROUGH IN THE COURSE OF ITS DAILY MOTION IN THE
HEAVENS as shown in the ephemeris for the current year.
The use of these significators will be given further on
in this exposition. FIRST, let us look at the method of
DIRECTING which has been found to be a guide TO THE GEN-
ERAL MARKET OUTLOOK.

The New York Chart is set for noon on the 17th of
May, 1792 as shown in the map herewith. Now at the tragic
assasination of President Abraham Lincoln we find the years
from the above date of founding to the date of that event,
APRIL 14TH, 1865, to be a period of 73 YEARS ONE MONTH.
This at the rate of 59' 8" per day (year) is 72 degrees
2 minutes and being added to the radical Midheaven of
Taurus 28 we come to the 11th degree of the sign LEO, AND.
THE ASCENDANT UNDER THIS M.C. is the 5th of SCORPIO. The
ascendant was therefore in opposition to Venus radical.
Refering to the ephemeris for 1865 we find that on that
very day Neptune, the author of plots and schemes, was in
Aries 8:40 and therefore exactly on the place of the Moon
radical.

AXIOM ONE

Planets in transit over the radical places of the
SUN, MOON, MIDHEAVEN, AND ASCENDANT OF THE CHART have in-

fluence on the course of events according to their natures, and so effect the VALUE OF SECURITIES. In November 1857 there was a considerable panic (financial panic) on the Exchange. Time 65 years 6 months. M.C. progress to Leo 2:34, Asc. in Libra 27. The Asc. is opposed to SATURN and in conjunction with NEPTUNE. VENUS was then in the end of LIBRA (CONJ. NEPTUNE r) and SATURN was in CANCER in square aspect to VENUS Midmonth in November 1857. URANUS was in transit over M.C. radical.

AXIOM TWO

DIRECTIONS OF THE GENERAL SIGNIFICATORS, SUN, MOON, M.C. AND ASC., TO AFFLICTING ASPECTS (SQUARE OR OPPOSITION) OF MALEFIC PLANETS WILL CAUSE GREAT DEPRESSION OF SECURITIES.

AXIOM THREE

The ephemeris aspects to the PRIME SIGNIFICATOR WILL DEFINE THE PROBABLE TIME FOR THIS DEPRESSION. The Railway Strike of August 1890 at 98 years 3 months from the foundation of the chart shows M.C. in Virgo 5. Saturn was then in transit through that degree of the Zodiac.

AXIOM FOUR

Saturn IN CONJUNCTION, OR SQUARE OR OPPOSITION-by transit-to ANY OF THE RADICAL PLACES OF THE GENERAL SIGNIFI-CATORS, OR TO THEIR PROGRESSED PLACES, WILL CAUSE A SERIES DEPRESSION. In August 1914 Saturn was in Gemini 28 in square to Mars in Virgo 28. The MC. of the chart had progressed to Virgo 28. Mars was therefore in transit over

the MC. Progressed and Saturn was in square to it. Mars
is here the cause of the excitement and Saturn that of
the Depression.

EFFECTS OF PLANETS. NEPTUNE in BAD ASPECT CAUSES BEAR
SALES AND ITS ACTION IS GENERALLY DUE TO "RINGS" AND
PROFESSIONAL COMBINES MOVING FOR A LOWER BUYING LEVEL.
ITS GOOD ASPECTS ADVANCE VALUES FROM THE SAME CAUSES.

URANUS USUALLY BRINGS IN THE GOVERNMENT BROKER AND
SHOWS OFFICIAL MANIPULATION OF THE MARKET. In good as-
pect it makes for buying, and in bad aspect for selling.
At such times keep one eye on URANUS and the other on the
Go vernment Broker.

SATURN steadies the market when in good aspect, but
greatly depresses it when in evil aspect to the SIGNIFICA-
TORS, RADICAL AND PROGRESSED.

JUPITER enhances values by its conjunction or good
aspects, and causes heavy selling for profits when in bad
aspect. It deflates what it previously had inflated.

MARS stimulates the market and in good aspect causes
sharp rises and a brisk market, while in evil aspect it
causes sharp depressions. Neither are enduring.

VENUS in good aspect gives equable values and a
steady rise in values but is not enduring. In bad aspect
it causes a flat and lifeless market.

MERCURY causes rises when in good aspect by 'reports'

and market talk and makes for brisk but small improvements.
In bad aspect it causes quick in and out buying and selling
with balance against values.

AXIOM

All planets in good aspect enhance values according
to their several natures, the major planets being more
powerful than the minor. Jupiter, Mars and Venus, have
the greatest power for good when in good aspect, but Venus
has not the same power in transit as in Direction.

THE DECANATES

Aries	0 to	10	Mars	11 to	20	Sun	21	to	30	Venus
Taurus	"		Merc	"		Moon	"			Saturn
Gemini	"		Jupiter			Mars	"			Sun
Cancer	"		Venus	"		Merc	"			Moon
Leo	"		Saturn	"		Jupiter	"			Merc
Virgo	"		Sun	"		Venus	"			Merc
Libra	"		Moon	"		Saturn	"			Jupiter
Scorpio	"		Mars	"		Sun	"			Venus
Sagit	"		Merc	"		Moon	"			Saturn
Capri	"		Jupiter	"		Mars	"			Sun
Aquarius	"		Venus	"		Merc	"			Moon
Pisces	"		Saturn	"		Jupiter	"			Mars

These decans are parts of signs each ten degrees in extent
and their rulers are set against them. When the PRIME
SIGNIFICATOR is passing through any decan it is the guest
of the ruler of that decan and is subject in some measure
to the aspects affecting that ruler so long as the PRIME
SIGNIFICATOR remains in that Decan. These can be found
in the ephemeris from week to week throughout the year and
FORM THE BASIS OF "FLUCTUATIONS", while being subject to the
general tone of the market indicated by the DIRECTIONS of

the general significators and the major transits over them.
For example:

At the time of the railway strike in 1890, we find
Saturn in transit over the M.C. Progressed in Virgo
5 and in square aspect to Mars, then in Sagittarius 5,
and near to square of Neptune in Gemi ni 6, while Uranus was in transit over Jupiter's place in the radix on
the cusp of the third house (Railways). But venus, the
PRIME SIGNIFICATOR, was then in the end of Virgo and
not in aspect to any planet in the heavens. The
Secondary Significator is Mercury, which rules the
last decan of Virgo, where Venus is guest. Now we
find Mercury was then in conjunction with Saturn in
Virgo 5 and therefore square to Mars and square to
Neptune in the heavens at the time. Here are adequate
causes for predicting a severe set-back.

NATURE OF ASPECTS

The good aspects are the trine of 120 degrees, the
sextile of 60 degrees, the conjunction of Jupiter and Venus
and the PARALLELS of these also. The bad aspects are the
opposition of 180 degrees, the square of 90, the sesq of
135, and the semi-square of 45. Also the conjunctions of
SATURN AND ITS PARALLELS. The planets URANUS, NEPTUNE,
AND MARS, ACT VARIOUSLY WHEN IN CONJUNCTION AND ARE LARGELY
UNDER THE DIRECTION OF PRIMARY INDICATIONS CURRENT AT THE TIME.

AXIOM

ALL PLANETS IN GOOD ASPECT ACT TO ENHANCE VALUES.
ALL PLANETS IN BAD ASPECT ACT TO DEPRECIATE VALUES.
BUT JUPITER IS THE GREATEST EXPANDER, AND SATURN THE
GREATEST DEPRESSOR OF THE MARKETS.

AXIOM

A PLANET IS JUDGED BY ITS OWN NATURE, AND AN ASPECT
BY ITS OWN NATURE.

A BOOM on the market is produced from a succession of
good aspects to the PRIME SIGNIFICATOR OR ITS DECAN RULER.
WHEN BOTH ARE WELL ASPECTED THE EXTENT IS DOUBLED. It is
usually terminated by a change of decan, if not sooner by
a break of benefic causes.

A SLUMP is caused by a succession of bad aspects to the
Significator and its Decan Ruler

TRANSITION POINTS are formed midway between a good
and a bad aspect to the same indicator. Thus:
Venus on the 8th of the month is opposition Jupiter.
On the 11th is sextile Saturn.
On the 20th it is semi-square Mercury.
On the 30th it is semi-square Neptune.

Therefore we should expect a fair amount of selling
or realizing of profits. This would be followed, about
the 9th or 10th, by a steadying influence under the ap-

proaching sextile of Saturn and Saturn would give a steady
upward trend until the 15th-16th, which is the transition
point between Saturn and the next aspecting planet Mercury.
At this time the market turns and begins to be talked down,
and under Venus semi-square Neptune it continues down to
the 28th. Here it forms another transition point and pro-
ceeds to the sextile of Mercury, which it reaches on August 2nd. These aspects are formed in July 1914. After
the 2nd of August the planet venus meets the conjunction
with Mars in Virgo on the 5th, and then goes to the square
of Saturn, the change of Decan taking place on August 2nd
and changing the good influence of Mercury to that of Mars
(war). Venus, being then in the last decan of Virgo, ruled
by Mercury, we have further indication of Mercury conjunction Neptune at that time, showing a state of chaos. The
direction for 122 years 3 months is 120 degrees 29 minutes
and it will be seen that if we add this amount to the M.C.
of the radix (Taurus 28) we arrive at just this same position in the zodiac, namely Virgo 28, which is occupied
by Mars and Venus in square aspect to Saturn in Gemini at
that time. So we have good reason for anticipating a considerable stir in the markets of the world and a great depreciation of values.

DAILY FLUCTUATIONS   CAN ONLY BE FOLLOWED WITH SUCCESS
by those who are on the spot and watching the clock and
ticker.   For it will be found that the course of the market follows the MERIDIAN TRANSIT of the planets and the
aspects formed to them by the other at the time of their
transit. Taking the Sun as indicating noon position, it
will be seen that some planets precede the Sun and others
follow it.   Thus at the beginning of August 1914 we have
Sun opposition Uranus, on the 2nd of the month, followed
by the Sun semi-square Saturn on the 6th.   The heaviest
point should therefore be on the 4th, or mid-distance between the aspects. On that date Mercury passed over the
MERIDIAN 19 degrees, or 1 hour 16 minutes before noon, in
opposition at the time to the Moon.   About 24 minutes later
Nepturne passed the MERIDIAN.   Then cam the Sun at Noon in
Opposition to Uranus and approaching the semi-square of
Saturn. Here we have the big depression. It is followed
by the transit of Jupiter over the lower Meridian at 12:28
or 28 minutes after noon. Then there is a lot of selling
done. Then comes Mars and Venus, in close conjunction in
Virgo 23-24 degrees in sextile to Mercury in Cancer 22, but
also coming to the square of Saturn in Gemini. This would
be about 3:50 P.M. Local Time, and it then became a press-
ing question as to Peace or War -- Mars or Venus -- question that would serve no market any good.

THE CHART OF ANY PRIVATE COMPANY OR SYNDICATE is to be judged by exactly the same set of indications, and the share values of such company, if offered on the open market, will follow the specific indications belonging to and derived from that chart, subject only to the general indications of the Exchange Chart and the ephemeral transits as already set forth. But each set of indications must be taken account of in THIS ORDER:

1. PRIMARY INDICATIONS, derived from directions of the Midheaven, etc for the current year.

2. TRANSITS OVER THESE PRIMARY POINTS - Sun, Moon, Midheaven, Asc., both radical and progressed, the latter being the more important in relation to the current period.

3. ASPECTS FORMED TO THE PRIME SIGNIFICATOR in the ephemeris from day to day or from week to week, as the case may be.

4. ASPECTS FORMED TO THE RULER OF THE DECAN THEN HELD BY THE PRIME SIGNIFICATOR.

All of these, which being duly noted, will form a concatenation or depending series of influences which will inevitably lead to correct estimate of the TREND OF THE MARKET.

5. Having decided to buy or sell, enter the market WHEN THE MERIDIAN TRANSITS ARE AGREEABLE TO THE CURRENT INDICATIONS FROM WHICH YOUR DECISION WAS MADE. This is the whole business of stock and share trading by chart.

SIGN RULERS

The Sun being in Capri or Aquar - - Saturn is Prime Sig.
The Sun being in Sagit or Pisces - Jupiter is Prime Sig.
The Sun being in Libra or Taurus - Venus is P. S.
The Sun being in Virgo or Gemini - Mercury is P. S.
The Sun being in Leo   - Sun is P.S.
The Sun being in Cancer - - - - - - Moon is P.S.

When the Moon becomes the P.S. through the Sun being in
the sign Cancer, as happens from Midsummer Day onwards for
a month, it is obvious that we cannot trace primary indications from the ephemeral aspects of so fast and variable a
body as the Moon, so what is to be done? Experience says,
Watch the position and aspect of the ASCENDING NODES of
the Moon, which is given for the second and third day continuously throughout the year in any good ephemeris. Merely
trace the node as if it were the Moon itself and the rest
follows in due sequence.

A few tests of the early July charts will show how
this works out. The NODE OF THE EARTH IS ALWAYS THE VERNAL
EQUINOX, AND ALWAYS ZERO ARIES. BUT THE NODE OF THE MOON
FROM WHICH ITS COURSE BEGINS, IS ONLY IN THE SAME LONGITUDE
AFTER A PERIOD OF 19 YEARS. The node thus becomes a very
important indicator. At the beginning of August 1914 it was
in Pisces 7 and had no aspects. But it was then in the Decan
of Saturn, and Saturn had a succession of bad aspects all
through the first three weeks of that month, so that Can-
cerian Charts were under evil aspects at that time.

It will be observed that there is a line of sympathy
between the New York and British Charts in that Venus is

the common PRIME SIGNIFICATOR. In the New York Chart it
is strong in its own sign Taurus and this perhaps accounts
for the strong Hibernian affinity. In the British Chart
(London) Venus is elevated in the Sign Gemini, which is
the ruling sign of the USA as a Republic. Consequently
there is much sympathy of action between the two markets,
and the coincidence of the midheaven degree is remarkable.
It is not inappropriate either that the Moon in the NY Chart
should be in the ruling sign of England, its P.S. in the
ruling sign of Ireland, and Fortuna in the ruling sign of
Scotland.

FORTUNA indicates the POSITION OF THE MOON AT THE TIME
OF LOCAL SUNRISE FOR ANY SET DATE. IT IS MEASURED BY LONG-
ITUDE, i.e., degrees and minutes of the zodiac.

THE COMPANY. In the case of a company, the M.C. is
THE CHAIRMAN, THE 11th HOUSE DENOTES THE DIRECTORS OR
BOARD OF CONTROL, THE ASCENDANT DENOTES THE SHAREHOLDERS.
THE SIXTH HOUSE SHOWS THE EMPLOYEES.

SPECIFIC HOUSE INDICATION.

THE FIRST HOUSE governs the PUBLIC in which is vested
all forms of enterprise and development.

THE SECOND HOUSE relates to PRICE OF MONEY, TRADE,
RETURNS, BULLION IMPORTS, BILLS OF EXCHANGE, ETC.

THE THIRD HOUSE rules railroads, tramways, omnibuses,
traction of all sorts, locomotion, telephone, aircraft,

canals, bridges and transports as well as postal service and all means of communication.

THE FOURTH HOUSE rules real estate, land explorations, mines, developements, crops, produce of raw material from the soil.

THE FIFTH HOUSE shows educational matters, art, theatres, cinemas, amusements and schools.

THE SIXTH HOUSE governs foodstuffs, clothing, equipment, outfitting supplies, upholstering, furnishings, building and upfitting.

THE SEVENTH HOUSE rules accountancy, banking, corporations, exchanges, contracts, equity, discounting, surveying, valuations, probate, etc.

THE EIGHTH HOUSE controls waste products, conservancy, dredging, petrol, parafine, benzine, medical accessories, chemicals and nitrates.

THE NINTH HOUSE is connected with insurance, cables, publishing, wireless, radiographs, liners and foreign affairs.

THE TENTH HOUSE rules state affairs, the government and political activity generally.

THE ELEVENTH HOUSE rules the Exchequer, bonds, government loans, electric and gaslight companies.

THE TWELFTH HOUSE rules laundries, breweries, fisheries boot mfgrs, hosiery and COLD STORAGE.

THE CHART OF THE HEAVENS FOR LONDON.

This is introduced in order to display the influence of ECLIPSES when falling on the places of the significators, either radical or progressed.

On the 12th of March 1914, there was an exlipse of the Moon which fell in Virgo 21. Incidentally, it happened to be in opposition to the ex-Kaiser's radical M.C. in Pisces 21. But what is more pertinent to our present study is the fact that Virgo 21 was the progressed M.C. for the London Exchange for the year 1914. Thus 59" 8' daily mean motion of the Sun, multiplied by 113, the years elapsed since 1801, gives 111 deg. 26 min., or 3 signs, 21 degrees, 26 min. This being added to the MC of the radix, Taurus 28, gives Virgo 20 on the MC for 1914.

Now Mars passed over the line of the eclipse in Virgo 20 on the 28-29th of July of that year and was was declared against Serbia by Austria on the 28th. On the 31st a state of war was declared in Germany, who declared war on Russia on the 31st or 1st of August and invaded Luxenbourg on the same date, French territory being invaded on August 2nd. This war and the exact date of it was forseen by "Sepharial" and notified by him in print throughout the country as early as July 1913.

Here we see how the meridian line of the Exchange horoscope, affecting all securities, was brought into line

with the eclipse which immediately preceded the Great War,
and how both were brought into line with the meridian of
the ex-Kaiser's horoscope. These considerations determined
the prediction of War and the date was defined by the transit of Mars over this triple combine of Virgo Pisces meridian.

The fiscal troubles which have dominated all British
politics arose from the eclipse of the meridian degree for
the year 1914, and its effects could be traced right through
to 1918, when, as early as August 1st, 1914, "Sepharial"
fixed the end of the war in these words: "The war will
be Titanic and will last until 1918" ---
The Hohenzollerns will bite the dust and gather the DEAD
SEA fruit of an inordinate ambition."

When for the last time in the period of 4 years (dura-
tion of eclipse) Mars was in transit over the same point,
Virgo 20, on March 21st, 1918, Germany launched its last
great offensive. America was then well represented at
the front and brought new blood into the conflict which
was steadily wearing out the reserves of Germany. It was
then said: "Hostilities will cease in November of this
year." By adding the increment of mean motion for 4 years
(1914-1918) to Virgo 20, we reach Virgo 24, and under this
meridian in the latitude of Longon we find Scorpio 29:24
to be rising. This is in 60 degrees aspect to Jupiter, with
a following 60 of the Moon in the radix, and this was follow-

KEY TO SUGAR VALUES

BY

SEPHARIAL

PRINCIPLES.

The following Key to Sugar Future Values is based upon the observed action of the planets upon one another in respect to the Earth as the common center of such interaction. The places of planets are such as are found in the current Ephemeris for the year under survey.

THE SUGAR TRADE.

The sugar trade is divided primarily into two sections indicated by the sort of sugar dealt in. Various descriptions of cane sugar are to be found in the ancient classics of the East and Middle East, and show that the industry was in full swing many centuries before it came to be known as an article of commerce in the West. In the Hanava Sha'stra of India there are frequent references to the use of sugar. Primarily, it was indigenous to India, Cochin China and the Malay Archepalago, and is found more or less widely distributed throughout the Tropics and sub-tropical countries, warmth and moisture being the essential conditions for sugar production, it was found that ideal conditions existed in the West Indies, Cuba and British Guinana, where it has been extensively cultivated. So far as European production is concern-ed, sugar appears to have been first imported to Cyprus (A. D. 1420) and thence was carried to Madiera, the Canary Islands, Brazil, Bar-badoes, and so spread throughout central and south American and the West Indies.

The varieties best known and in most common use are Maple Sugar, Palm Sugar and Cane Sugar. The latter is the most considerable indust-ry and controls the chief markets. Up to the end of the 18th century it was the staple article.

CANE SUGAR

This article is under the direct influence of the planet Mars. It is described as the "Indian Honey-bearing Reed" by Strabo XV 1.20, and this is perhaps the first classical reference to the article in the West. As a constituent of food it represents the ideal heat-producing element, and thus is correctly ascribed to the planet Mars. But while the article itself is controlled from Mars, its external qualities and its market value is controlled by Venus. Thus the Ascendant being in Aries it is under the dominion of Mars, but the 2nd House determines its value, and this is ruled by Taurus, the sign of Venus. This exactly answers the known qualities of the article, for while it is itself a great organic caloric, its external nature is dulcent, mellient and sweetly soothing.

Therefore in tracing the market in Cane sugar we have to determine the plenitude or scarcity of supplies by the position and aspects of Mars, but in tracing the market fluctuations of price we have to follow the perturbations of Venus.

The industry shows a variety of values attaching to the canes, according to their sugar-bearing properties. Thus canes yielding 6 % sugar (mixed qualities) commands 6/8 per ton, those yielding 7 % being valued at 7/9 per ton, and those yielding 15 ⁒ fetching 10/ per ton, in English money. Of every 1000 tons of canes crushed, some 622 tons is evaporated, the resultant masscuit being about 126 tons, the sugar yield being about 100 tons. The value of the yield in normal times was about £ 8 per ton.

BEET SUGAR

The industry in this article arose in Germany from the experiments of Marggraff of Berlin. He treated the juice of beetroot with alcohol and extracted 6.2 ⁒ of sugar from the white beet, and 4.5 ⁒ from the red beet.

The industry soon became very extensive and was carried to France where ideal soil conditions were available. But for a considerable time Germany produced 12.79 % of beet sugar to France's 11.5 %. Intensive culture of beet under Lord Donbigh on his estate at Newnham Paddox, produced 15.5 % of sugar juice from a crop of beet averaging 25.5 tons to the acre. Those surprising results were reached in the year 1910. In general it may be said that one ton of beetroot is equivalent of one ton of canes.

Beet sugar now largely supplants the cane sugar on the world's markets and is increasingly in demand, as the following figures will show.

THE WORLD'S TRADE

In 1840 the total world's supply was 1 million tons, of which 50,000 were beet sugar, the average price being 48/- per cwt.

In 1850 the total was 1,400,000 tons, of which 200,000 were beet and the average price per hundredweight was 40/-.

In 1860 the total was 1,899,000 tons of which 389,000 were beet, the average price being 35/- per cwt.

In 1870 the total was 2,416,000 tons, of which 831,000 were beet, the average price being 32/- per cwt.

In 1880 the total trade was 3,659,000 tons, of which 1,748,000 were beet, the average price being 20/4 per cwt.

It will thus be seen that the world's production and trade in sugar has increased enormously during the successive decades of the past century, and is still increasing at this date. But also it is seen that in proportion as the trade in beet sugar increases, the cost of the article diminishes, a clear proof that beet sugar is as readily produced as cane sugar and that its working is considerably cheaper. It is evidently intended to replace the trade in cane sorts for the reason that it can be produced in temperate climates and does not require special climactic conditions. An article that is grown, worked and sold on the spot where the trade is greatest, is bound to assume an ascendancy over all other sorts. The following figures in relation to BEET trade in sugar by the British Ports are in this respect very eloquent.

BRITISH REPORTS

1870	-	-	785,000 tons	-	- price 30/4 per cwt
1880	-	-	1,001,000 "	-	- 29/5
1890	-	-	1,285,000 "	-	- 16/4
1900	-	-	1,624,000 "	-	- 12/10

TRACKING THE MARKET

The equipment for this process is an ephemeris of the planet's places for the current year, and this can be obtained from my publishers, Messrs Foulsham and Co. Ltd through any agent or bookseller. Note the position and aspects of the planet Mars through any month and you will find that it responds to the market reports as to the supply of sugar.

When Mars is badly aspected the article will show a corresponding scarcity. The planet aspecting it at the time will gennerally indicate the cause of the restriction. Thus Saturn in square or opposition to Mars will show bad crop reports. Jupiter in bad aspect generally means that speculators have got the supplies in hand. Neptune simhliarly in aspect to Mars shows rings, cliques and trusts in operation, or a "corner" is formed in the article. Uranus in bad aspect restricts operations of dealers through Government buying or control, or some other action of the authorities at the ports or the factories. Supplies open out when Mars reaches itsaphelion in the early degrees of Virgo, and correspandingly are restricted when in perihelion in Pisces. Abnormal conditions may of course modify these rules.

Good aspects of the major planets to Mars in the ephemeris show easy supplies, the controlling conditions being similiar to those already recited in connection with the nature of the planet in aspect to Mars.

MARKET PRICES

Market prices of the article are controlled by the perturbations and affections of the planet Venus. This planet is strong in the signs Taurus, Cancer, Libra and Pisces. When thus placed and in good aspect to any of the major planets, the price will rise; and a proportionate increase in value will be noted when the planet is in any of the other signs, and in good aspect to major planets.

Venus is weak in Aries, Capricorn, Scorpio and Virgo. Good aspects to Venus will not then have the same value as if the planet were in a congenial sign, but evil aspects will have a more depressing effect.

Hence not only the sign occupied by Venus, but also the aspects thrown to itx by other planets have to be considered, and an estimate made accordingly.

THE CHART

The chart of Sugar should be laid down day by day throughout any month or year. The aspects to Mars should be noted and set against the day of the month on which they occur. This forms the base line of supply and greatly influences the market.

The aspects of Venus should then be similiarly noted and set down against the date of their fomation, any change of sign that may occur in the course of the chart being also indicated.

From these two lines of influences a curve can be set out which indicates the rise and fall of the article on the market.

Venus is in ephelion in Libra 10 degrees and in perihelion in Aries 10.

A BOOM

A boom on the market is caused by a succession of good aspects to the planet Venus, without any intervening bad aspect to break the series.

CHANGES

A change from up to down or the reverse is usually indicated by
Venus coming into conjunction with the Sun, but the more sure indication is a change in the nature of the ephemeral aspects to Venus.

Thus if you find a succession of sextiles or trines to Venus and
then a series of bad aspects or mixed ones, a change takes place when
the planet moves from one to the other of them. This is called a transition date.

TRANSITION DATES

A transition date is fixed by taking the date of the last good
aspects and the next bad aspect to Venus, counting the number of days
and dividing by two, which, being added to the first date, gives the
date of the transition. Similiarly a transition date will fall midway between the last bad aspect and the next good one.

An interval of at least four days between two sorts of aspects
should be allowed so that Venus may clear the last influence by its
ephemeral motion before entering upon the next.

SUPPLY AND DEMAND

Bring the primary conditions controlling any market and those
which determine the price of any article or product, we have only to
note that in normal times prices are in inverse proportion to the
supply. But this holds good up to a certain point only, for supply
cannot of itself create demand. Given peaceful industrial conditions
the world over, the world demand in sugar will very soon be satisfied and any surplus will tend to reduce the market price of the article. War conditions, crop failures and other abnormal conditions,
must be dealt with as they arise, and they will invariably be reflect-
ed in the sugar chart. For this reason we are able to say that sugar
will tend to strong waves from time to time during the next decade
(10 years), from 1920 to 1922, and from 1926 to 1931 more especially

these being well defined areas of world unrest and international war, just as the period from 1914 to 1918 was in its turn. These are refered to as artificial factors, and are arising from factors outside of the industry concerned, they have to be sought for from other sources. The best guide to Political prediction and forecast of War Periods is my key to Stocks and Shares, these being controlled from political causes rather than from natural causes. But in as much as Sugar is a staple article of food and of great industrial value the fact of its coming under "control" by the Government has the immediate effect of suspending all normal fluqtuations.

In otherrespects and in normal times this key will be found of great value to the dealer in buying or selling forward.

Sepharial

RUBBER

BY

SEPHARIAL

Rubber   The ruler is Jupiter.In ancient Indian scriptures
Jupiter is referred to as the "Lord of Expansion". Look to
Jupiter for the state of the Rubber Market.

The Apsides...of the planet Jupiter are defined by the
perihelion and aphelion of that body as Astronomically determined.
The perihelion was (1929) in 13   11' of the sign **Libra**,that is
to say,the planet when 193 11' from the Vernal Equinox is at
the point in the Orbit where it is nearest to the Sun. At
this time there is a considerable increase of the Solar Action
upon that planet and as the action is to expand,there is found
to be a considerable increase in the output at this period,
with correspondingly lower prices for the article,expansion of
trade,and a higher share value. On the other hand,when the planet
Jupiter is in Aries 13° it is at its greatest Orbittal distance
from the Sun,the effect being to decrease the output,reduce the
trading, and depreciate the share values.

Other causes may intervento produce appreciation or depreciation
of share values,but these are the natural and economic factors
and may be regarded as the foundations of the Rubber trade..

They are Nature's and man's response to celestial influences genera-
ted in the heavens.

The Orbit

of Jupiter is not Heliocentric but has an eccentricity of 5½ deg.,
by which space the center of Jupiter's orbit is removed from the

center of the Sun. This causes an irregularity of motion,
which is greatest when the planet is nearest to the Sun,
and least when it is furthest away. There is a half way point
between the A sides when the planet is at its mean distance
and when its motion is at its mean also:-
These problems play an important part when rubber values are to be
determined.
We find the lowest share values to be associated with the passage
of Jupiter over the aphelion, or furthest point from the Sun.
This happened in April 1922 when the mean value was at 18/-per
share.   By the end of February 1925,the planet had reached its
quadrature or mean distance in theOrbit and was coming nearer
to the Sun. Share values were then on the rise having already
reached the mean value of 28/-. As the planet came nearer to
the Sun,the value of shares increased, as already shown to be
expected, and in 1925-6 the mean value was 51/-/
The Perihelion is not reached until March 1928,when the influence
is at the maximum.

The Economic Factor..
Came into market play after the war.The various companies,which
are mainly financed by British capital,lost considerable custom

from countries which/hitherto benn buyers, and with
the abnormal supply of the article,this curtailment of
the demand for it caused a considerable fall off in
the price of the article,which became overstocked
in London. The Stevenson agreement reducted production to create scarsity for price increase.

          The Artifical Factor
This may arise from external sources,say political.
Hostilities would have an immediate effect in raising
the price of the commodity with while depressing the
value of shares, thus acting contrary to the economic
factor in that production would be speeded up and
would be rapidly absorbed,but excess in this direction would be offset by other factors, and the fiscal
position would be rendered insecure,the position would
induce to free selling of shares and consequent slump
on the market.

But apart from this artificial factor,there is poss-
ibility of seismic and other physical disasters.The
great rubber producing tract of the Strairs Settlements,
the Malay Archipelago are well defined earthquake area.

The artificial factors cannot be apprehended except by
constant touch with the sources of information, political
and meteorological which are concerned with them.

The VARIABLE FACTOR

Here we return once more to the perturbations of the
chief significator of the Rubber Industry Jupiter.
It has been found that in its Orbital course extending
over twelve years, its passage thru one sign of the Zodiac
in the course of a year gives rise to three distinct
phases of influence. These are controlled from the Decans,
or divisions of the Sign into three parts of ten degrees each.

Each Decan is ruled by a planet as:

Aries	Mars	Sun	Venus
Taurus	Merc	Moon	Saturn
Gemini	Jup	Mars	Sun
Cancer	Ven	Mer	Moon
Leo	Sat	Jup	Mars
Virgo	Sun	Ven	Merc
Libra	Moon	Sat	Jup
Scorpio	Mars	Sun	Ven
Sag	Merc	Moon	Sat
Cap	Jup	Mars	Sun
Aqua	Ven	Merc	Moon
Pisc	Sat	Jup	Mars

Perturbations

arise from the passage of Jupiter from one Decan to
another,by which it comes successively under the
domination of a different planet. Thus at the beginning
of 1929 Jupiter had just entered Taurus and is therefore in the first decan of ~~the~~ that sign, ruled by Mercury.
It continues in that Decan until the 16th of March.
During the whole of this period we have to watch the
aspects to the planet Mercury who imparts its influence
to the planet Jupiter.It is therefore necessary to list
the aspects of Mercury as they are formed between Jan.1st
and March 16th for this year.

They are:

Jan.10th Sext.Uranus

        12   Sesquare Mars

        14   Semisquare Saturn

        21   Semisquare Uranus

        31 Parallel Jupiter

Here we get a rising market to the 10th,changing on the
11th and goin lower under successive adverse indications
to a date midway between the 21st and 31st, which is the
26th.Then improving under the Parallel of Jupiter, and
thus ends the month,which closes steady to firm.

Feb 4th   △ ♂
    5th   ∠ ♅ P♃
    6th   ∠ ♀ P♃
    7th   ☌ ☉
    11th ∠ ♄
    15th ✳ ♀
    19th ∠ ♂
    25 Sesquare ♂ again due to the

Here we get indicatons for a firm market to the 4th, then
uncertain, then lower to the 11th or 12th, higher to 16th,
then lower to end of month.

March 2nd ∠ ♄
      8th P ♀
      9th ∠ ♅
      14   P ♃
      15   ☍ ♃
      16   ✳ ♄
      17   △ ♂

This is the limit of the Mercurial Decan of Taurus, and
we now pass to the Moon which rules the next Decan. When the
Moon, which is very swift in motion comes into play it
usually indicates an unsettled and variable market, very
active and liable to many ups and downs. It continues in
force until April 30th, and is succeeded by Saturn which
is then retrograde in the beginning of Capricorn and going
to
in the preceding sign Sagittarius on May 5th. Jupiter continues under the influence of Saturn's aspects to other
bodies until the 11th of June when it enters Gemini and
comes under the influence of its own aspects since it

it rules the first decan of that sign.In this Decan it
continues until the 30th of July and enters the Decan of
Mars on the 31st.The planet Jupiter then goes forward
as far as the 16th degree of Gemini,still under the
influence of Mars until the 5th of October,when it turns
back (retrograde) and recedes from the territory of Mars
on the 13th of December and comes into its own domain in the
sign Gemini on Dec.14th. Here it remains to the end of the
year.

Therefore we have successive indications throughout the
year,namely:

Jan 1 to Mar 16 — ☿
Mar 17 " Apr 30   ♂ (Watch aspects to Node)
Apr 30 " June 11 ♄
June 12 " July 30 ♃
July 31 " Dec 13 ♂, and then ♃ to the end of the year

SUMMARY NOTES

It will be observed that there is a general trend of the
market due to the position of the planet in its orbit.The
elements are as follows:

Jupiter in Perihelion (nearest to Sun)April 1922

Mean distance March 1925 in aphelion (farthest from Sun)

Feb.March 1928,mean distance Feb.1931, and then back
to Perihelion in 1934.Period 12 years.

It will be seen also that within these limits there are
many changes on indication due to the passage of Jupiter
from one sign to another in the course of 12 years (about
one sign per year), and also from one decan into another
in the course of the sign. that Hence we have a cyclic trend, a
major indication and a minor indication, and a right estimate
of these factors will induce to correct apprehension of the
Markets course.

Jupiter is strongest in Taurus,Cancer,Sagittarius and Pisces
than in other signs. It is more in harmony with Mars,the Sun,
Venus and the Moon than other Decan rulers, and is therefore
disposed to greater strength when in these decans.

All bad aspects to the current indicator depress the market,
and all good aspects raise it, a succession of good aspects
uninterrupted by bad ones will produce a boom. A succession of
unbroken bad aspects to the Decan Significator will bring a
slump. Mixed aspects in alternation will produce fluctuations.
The influence of one planetary aspect to the Decan ruler will
last until a date midway between its own aspect and the next in
succession. When the Moon is the Significator of the decan,the
aspects to the Node should be watched for fluctuations.

THE MASTER KEY

BY

SEPHARIAL

THE MASTER KEY

by

Sepharial.

The Map for the event is simply set by adding to time of the event the SIDEREAL TIME at noon. Correct the result by adding or subtracting Local Time. Subtract for West, add for East, of Greenwich. Find the sign and degree from the Table of Houses for the Midheaven or 10th House of your map. The other Cusps will have the same degree of the successive signs upon them so that the Signs are equally distributed through the Houses. This is called the Universal Key or Horoscope. Put in the places of the Sun, Moon and Fortuna, to the nearest degree.

Planets Places

These are only required when they happen to fall exactly on the cusp of a House, or in the degrees next that which is on the Cusp. Thus: If the Cusp be 23° of a Sign, then any planet that is 23 to 28° of a Sign, must be placed in the Map according to its longitude, which is only required to the nearest whole degree.

Cuspal Indications

It is found that the Cuspal Indications are the strongest positions and any planet that is on or near the cusp is capable of figuring in the result of a race, hence they are called Indications. BUT, inasmuch as events are usually decided some minutes after the time for which they are set, a planet that is applying to a cusp and within 5° of it has more to do with the result than one which is on the cusp at the set time, for every four minutes of time will bring a new or different degree on to the cusp and one that is exactly on the Cusp at the set time of the race is usually waning, or getting weaker by the time the Race is run, whereas a planet that is coming to the cusp will be at its full strength at the finish or decisive moment.

Consequently you must look for a planet that is coming to a cusp of a house, and if there be more then one, take the one that is nearest.

The Sun, Moon and Fortuna, are to be regarded as planets in the sense that they may be on or near a Cusp and thus be Indicators.

Note that when there is a planet exactly on a cusp, and none other within orbs of a cusp (5°) then the Cuspal Indications must be taken.

This rule seems to hold good even when the race is many minutes late in starting. The fact appears to be that all competitors or horses must be out of the paddock at the official starting time. Therefore the SET TIME is that which determines the event and not the time of the finish.

Astrology is supposed to see the end from the beginning.

Support is given to a significator when it is in line with another planet, especially in line with Fortuna, by being in line is meant either in conjunction or in Mundane Parallel - that is the same distance from the Midheaven or horizon - thus Mars on the cusp of the 11th house would be in line with Fortuna on the cusp of the 3rd house, in parallel to another planet on the cusp of the 9th house, and of course, in conjunction or line with Fortuna, this seldom fails to indicate the weight of the winner.

When planets are in opposition - that is - in the same degree of opposite signs or nearly so, they produce:

Transverse Polarity

If we find a planet on the cusp of the 3rd house, in opposition to a planet on the cusp of the 9th house, they produce a Polarity between them, and a Transverse Polarity between the cusps of the 6th and 12th houses, which are at right angles to them, the cusps have to be taken as if the planets were there, and the indication measured. While if there be actually a planet where planets in opposition from the Midheaven and Nadir throw off to the Ascendant and a planet which is then rising or setting will indicate the winner, but if there is no such planet to take up the Polar of the opposing Planets, they have to be taken as cuspal Indications only, and being opposed, they are weak, so that if there be a single other indication, it can win off them.

The Measure.

The scale is the difference between the top and bottom weights reduced to pounds. The measure in every case is one sixth of the scale of weights and this is the weight due to each of the houses above and below the horizon.

Distribution.

The extension of the scale of weights is thus applied. The Ascendant shows the top weights, the 4th house the middle weight and the 7th house the bottom weight.

By Alteration...

The 7th House shows the top weight the 10th the middle weight, and the Ascendant the bottom weight. The same rule holds good with regard to the other houses, hence it will be seen that each house denotes two weights, one which is as much from the top of the scale as the other is from the bottom, and these two weights added together, amount to the sum of the top and bottom weights, consequently, if we distribute the scale evenly through the houses, marking the cusp with the weights to which they correspond in the scale, we shall find that any indicator on or near a cusp shows two weights and these weights are found to be the same, or the nearest to the weight carried by the winner, and placed horses in over 80% taking both.

This is from a sustained analysis of reaults extending over 11 years.

These are all the rules to observe, and how easy to apply and how convincing in effect, may be judged from examples of past racing.

It is, of course, open to the student to trace results through past racing results with the aid of the Ephemeris for any year, and by careful study of the examples given here.

EXAMPLES

Example 1   27th March, 1906, at 3.20 p.m.

Taurus is on the Midheaven. None of the Planets are within orbs of and applying to the cusps. The Moon was in Taurus 5° and the Sun in Aries 6°, therefore Fortuna is seen to be 29° from the Ascendant, and applying to the cusp of the 2nd house.
The scale of Weights, top 8.8, - bottom 6.0 or 36lbs, and one sixth of this is 6 lbs, which is the Measure of one house. Fortuna being on the cusp of the 2nd house is 6 lb. for top and bottom weight of the runners.

Top.	8 st. 8 lbs.	
Bottom.	6 st. 0 lbs.	
	2 st. 8 lbs =36lbs.	6 divided by 36 = 6 lbs

Deduct 6 lbs from 8 st 8 lbs, leaving 8 st. 2 lbs. Add 6 lbs to 6 st. making 6 st. 6 lbs.

The Winner was Ob, which carried 8 stone at 100 to 7 against. 8 stone was the nearest weight to the indicated weight, 8 st. 2lbs. Note the progress of Fortuna depends on that of the Moon in relation to the Sun, therefore its progress through the houses is in the numerical order of the houses.

Example 2   19th March, 1907 at 3.20 pm.

Lincoln H/p. Scale 9.3 - 6 st. difference 45 lbs.
Measure 7½ lbs. The Midheaven was Taurus 18°. Mars was 5° from the cusp of the 5th house. Fortuna 64° from the Ascendant and therefore leaving the cusp of the 3rd house. This is one house, or 7½ lbs and taking this from the top weight 9.3 we get 8 st. 9½lbs. The nearest weight was Ob, who won this event last year. The price was 25 to 1.

Example 3 23rd March 1907   The Grand National.

The Midheaven was 19°. Uranus leaving the cusp of the 6th house. Moon 18° approaching the cusp of 12th house in Cancer. Saturn 19° approaching the cusp off the 8th house in Pisces 19°. Hence Saturn and the Moon were supporting one another being at equal distance from the Midheaven, and both at the distance of one house or 30° from the Horizon. Scale 12 st. 7 lbs - 9 st. 7 lbs. Difference 42 lbs. One sixth of 42 is 7 lbs, added to bottom weight gives 10 st. Nearest was Eremon, 10 st. 1 lb.

Example 4   23rd April. 3.15. The Great Metropolitan Stakes.

Midheaven Gemini 20°. Saturn and Venus applying and within 5° of the cusp. They are nearly in conjunction and setting. Fortune was 122° from the Ascendant, therefore leaving the cusp of the 5th house while the above planets were applying to the cusp of the 7th house.
Hence we say Top or Bottom is due to win. Scale Mintagoe 8 st. 11 lbs. Father Blind 6 at. 2 lbs. Winner Father Blind, 20 to 1.

Example 5 24th April, 3.15 pm.   City and Suburban.

Saturn and Venus applying to the Cusp of the 7th House, T or B to win, Velocity 9 st. 2lbs. Kolo 6 at. 2 lbs. Kolo making the running fell, and Velocity coming on behind jumped over Kolo and won. Winner Velocity 6 to 1.

Example 6   Manchester. August 4th 1917 . Race 2.0 pm. summer time.

Leo 23° was on the Midheaven. The Sun and Moon are working together, being at the same distance from the Angles to within 4°. No Planets are on the cusps. The Sun's distance from the west horizon is 79°, and the Moon's distance 83°, the average of this is about 80 or 81°. Scale 9.0 - 7.12 equals 16 lbs. 81° gives 7 lbs. This added to the B. W. gives 8. 5. Winner Op (Ob?) 3 to 1 8 st. 4 lbs.

Example 7   Race 1.40. Manchester, August 4th 1917.

Midheaven. Virgo 3 degrees. Scale 9 st. 7 lbs - 8 st. 4 lbs. Diff. 17 lbs. The Measure of each house is 3 lbs. Mercury held the Midheaven in opposition to the Moon. These threw off polarity to the cusps of the 1st and 7th house, here we find Jupiter setting, and only 4° from the cusp of the horizon, and therefore operative.
Top or bottom to win. Top weight won.

Example 8   Manchester. August 6th. Race 1.40 pm.

Virgo 6° on the Midheaven.   Saturn and Neptune were nearing the cusp of the 9th house in Leo 5° and the Moon was leaving the cusp of the 5th house in Aries 1°, therefore the Moon, Saturn and Neptune were acting together, they were two houses from the horizon. Scale 9 st 0 lbs - 6 st 10 lbs. Difference 32 lbs and the Measure is 11 lbs for two houses. This added to the bottom weight gives 7.7. nearest to this weight is 7 st 9 lbs carried by the winner, Puro.

Example 9 Manchester. August 6th 1917. 2.15 pm. Manchester Cup.

Virgo 15° on the Midheaven. No planets applying to cusps except Uranus in Aquarius 22° on the cusp of the 3rd house. This gives two houses from the horizon. Scale 8 st. 11 lbs. - 7 st 1 lb. Difference 24 lbs. and for two houses. This gives 8 lbs. which when added to the bottom weight gives 7 st. 9 lbs, the exact weight carried by the winner, Blue Danube.

Example 10 15th August 1917. Race 2 o'clock.

Midheaven Virgo 23°. Sun on the cusp of the 9th house opposed to Uranus on the cusp of the 3rd house - hence we look for polarity to the cusps of the 6th and 12th houses. There are no planets to take up the Transverse Polarity and therefore, we regard them as single indicators. Two houses from the horizon will therefore be the Measure. Scale 9 st. 0 lb. - 7 st. 6 lbs. Difference 22 lbs. and two houses gives 7 lbs which taken from the top weight gives the weight of the winner, My Ronald.

Example 11 16th April, 1918. Race 3.50 pm.

Midheaven Gemini 18•. No planets on cusps. The Moon was 70• from Horizon and Fortuna 72• - hence they were acting together. BUT NOTE that the Sun was 52• from the Midheaven and Saturn 50• on the other side of it and both above the horizon and therefore parallel. The average gives 51•, which gives 8 lbs. which added to the bottom weight gives 6 st. 1 lb. Wallrock, the winner carried 6 st. 3 lbs. Another light weight carried 5 st. 13 lbs. which ran second (White Nile). This clearly shows that planets in parallel work together, and the nearest to a cusp wins. The Sun and Saturn were in this case nearer to a cusp than the Moon and Fortuna.

This system is deemed to be the final word in Racing Systems. It embodies the result of 11 years of observation and research and is itself the easiest and most reliable of the many attempts that have been made to fathom the profundities of racing problems and it is claimed that the Master Key leaves others behind and gives the best results.

You will find that the master Key is really simple to work and requires only a surface knowledge of Astrology.

THE GOLDEN KEY

BY

SEPHARIAL

"The Golden Key" by Sepharial (Walter Gorn Old)
From a hand written copy

The basis of the system (without an astrological map) is the relationship of 40° to 360°.

The 40th part of the circle is equal to 9°, called a "Node".

The nodal measure at which the influence vested in that measure becomes operative, (9 times 9, or 81,) is the extent of that measure.

These points of nines are positive and negative terminals called "Nonal Degrees".

In practice the negative terminals only account for 20% of winners, so are generally ignored.

The positive degrees are:	Root	The negative degrees are
72°	81°	63°
54°		45°
36°		27°
18°	Zero 0°	9°

Therefore the standard values are for practical purposes, 18° 36° 72° 81° with an eye on 0° = bottom weight.

The proportion of the scale is one tenth.

To get the 1/10th of the scale of weights - move the last figure to a decimal point: then multiply the 1/10th by 1. 2. 3. 4. 4.5. (four and a half).
Call the answer lbs: take from the top weight and add to the bottom weight.

(1/10th x 1 = 18, 1/10th x 2 = 36, 1/10th x 3 = 54, 1/10th by 4 = 72, 1/10th x 4.5 = 81 Nodal.)

Example: Top weight = 10st 7lbs, bottom weight = 7st 7lbs
10st 7lbs - 7st 7lbs = 3st, ie 42lbs therefore scale = 42lbs.
Divide scale by 1/10th = 4lbs

So from the above we have 10 weights - though they may not all fit a weight carried exactly.

If more than one is exact we proceed with a check method to reduce these to one weight.

The first check method is as follows:

1. If the scale of weights equals an even number, deduct 4lbs.
2. If the scale of weights is an odd number, deduct 3lbs.
3. Divide the scale by 2 and call it the "Fulcrum Weight".
4. Take this from the top weight and add to the bottom weight.
The top half is called the "Heavy Fulcrum", the lower half the "Light Fulcrum".

Example: 42lbs is 4+2 = 6, an even number. 42 - 4 = 38/2 =19lbs leverage.

19lbs from 10st 7 = 9st 2lbs.   19lbs to 7st 7 = 8st 12lbs

Any weight confirming exactly a weight found by the first process is the selection.

If no single selection is found, then proceed to the next check method:

1. To the Heavy Fulcrum, add 5lbs: 3lbs: 5lbs: 3lbs until the top weight is reached.
2. To the Light Fulcrum, deduct 5lbs: 3lbs: 5lbs: 3lbs until the bottom weight is reached.

Heavy Fulcrum		Light Fulcrum	
9st	2lbs	8st	12lbs
+5 = 9	7	-5 = 8	7
+3= 9	10	-3 = 8	4
+5= 10	1	-5 = 7	13
+3= 10	4	-3 = 7	10

If more than one weight is still indicated, proceed to the next check method:

1. Reduce the scale, as in the first check method, by 4 if an even number and by 3 if odd.
2. Halve the scale and call R/2.
3. From R/2 deduct 7 as often as possible and the remainder (less than 7) gives a number we call 1st terminal point in lbs.
4. That point is developed or extended by adding to the bottom weight, then adding 3lbs: 4lbs: 3lbs: 4lbs successively until the scale is covered and note which of these weights confirm the Nonal weight.

Example:
19lbs/7 = 2 and 5 over. Call 5 the terminal.
Add to bottom weight 7st 7lbs + 5 = 7st 12lbs.
To this weight add 3lbs: 4lbs: 3lbs: 4lbs until top weight is reached.

Thus by these check methods the weights are often reduced to a single selection.

This system is based on the numerical value of planets to astrology without the necessity of drawing and judging a map.

THE ECLIPSE SYSTEM

BY

SEPHARIAL

Principles

It has been shown in the Golden Key, The Universal Key and the Lunar Key systems that the Sun, Moon and Part of Fortune can all be used separately and under certain conditions as a factor indicating the winner, it being at the same time obvious to the student that there is no guaranteed continuity. That at one time the Sun may be the Significator of the event, at another the Moon, and so on. The Eclipse system now determines once and for all when one factor is Significator and when another may be and this by a simple rule. It also shows why at one time the measure is direct and at another, converse.

In effect the Eclipse System is the answer to the outstanding problem of all racing systems. To reduce this to practise, the first thing is...

Setting the Figure

This is extremely simple. It consists merely in finding the degree that is on the Midheaven at the schedule or programme time of a race. The other cusps of the houses will hold the same degree and the signs will be equally disposed throughout the circle. Thus if Leo 23 were on the Midheaven then Scorpio 23 would be rising.

The Sun and Moon are placed in the figure to the nearest degree. The Part of Fortune is also placed in the figure. It is calculated thus:

From the longitude of the Moon (expressed in signs and degrees) adding 12 signs if necessary for subtraction, take the longitude of the Sun and add the longitude of the Ascendant. The result is the longitude in signs and degrees counted from Aries 0, of the Part of Fortune, called Fortuna.

With these simple elements and the weights of the runners you may proceed at once to find the...

Significator

which is always that factor (Sun, Moon or Fortuna) which is NEAREST to the cusp of a house.

The Measure...

The measure of the Significator is its distance from the nearest angle, the angles being the Midheaven, Nadir, Ascendant and Descendant. The converse measure is the difference between the Measure and 90°, or in other words its distance from the further angle.

The Scale...

of weights is the difference between the top and bottom weights of the runners reduced to lbs. As 9.0 - 6.0 = 42 lbs. In this system we use only half the scale which is always equal to 90°.

Heavy and Light...

weights are distinguished by the Middle weight, which is always half the sum of the top and bottom weights. Weights above it are heavy and those below it are light. The Measure of the Significator is applied normally to the top weight to get the heavy weight indication and the compliment or converse measure is applied to the bottom weight to get the light weight indication. But there is an exception to this which will be indicated.

Proportion...

is effected by multiplying half the scale of weights by the Measure and dividing by 90. Thus if the Measure were 25 degrees and the Scale of weights were 42 lbs. then we multiply 25 by 21 (half 42) and divide by 90 which gives 6 lbs. nearly, to be taken from the top weight of runners. Now take 6 lbs. from half the Scale and we get 15 lbs to be added to the bottom weight. By this means we get the indicated heavy and light weights due to the Significator.

Direct and Converse...

measure may now be illustrated. When the Significator is supported by either of the other factors (Sun Moon or Fortuna) by those factors indicating the same weights or horses, then it is a sure winner. But when both the other factors (NEITHER being the Significator) show the same weights as one another, and different weights to the Significator, then they act together and instead of destroying the significance of the other factor or Significator they reverse its terms so that we have to apply the measure from the nearest angle to the bottom weight instead of to the top and the converse measure to the top weight instead of the bottom. If we call the short measure A and the long measure B, then in normal cases A is applied to the top weight and B to bottom weight to get the INDICATED weights. But in converse or abnormal cases, B is applied to the top and A to the bottom. But in no case do we ever take the measures from any other than the prime factor which is the Significator.

Examples

The following consecutive events are taken from recent racing, but those who study the records of 1915 and 1916 will be satisfied that these are not "selected" examples.

Manchester

August 4th 1917 1.0 pm (This is Sun time or Greenwich Mean Time which is one hour earlier than "Summer Time")   Sidereal time at noon 8.50, less 10 mins for west longitude - gives 8.40 and to this we add the true time 1.0 pm and get 9.40 as the sidereal time for the Midheaven at Manchester. This gives Midheaven in Leo 23° - Sun in Leo 12° - Moon in Pisces 0° - Fortuna in Gemini 11°.

From these positions we get the cuspal distances Sun 11° Moon 7° Fortuna 12°. The Moon being the NEAREST to a cusp is the SIGNIFICATOR. It's distance from the nearest angle is the same as from the cusp, namely 7° and the converse measure is 83°. The scale was 9.0 - 7.12 or 16, half of which is 8 lbs. Multiply 8 by 7 and divide by 90. This being more than half a lb. we call one lb. and take it from the top weight, thus getting 8.13 as the indicated weight. Also we find that 8 less one is 7 lbs. which we add to the bottom weight, thus getting 8.5 as the other or alternate indicated weight.
Result

There was no 8.13 in the race but the nearest to it was top weight and ran second. There was no 8.5 in the race but the nearest to it was 8.4 TAGRAG, who won. Note that the Sun supported the Moon by indicating the same weights and therefore it was a certainty. Note: Always follow the horse nearest the indicated weight.
Same day at 1.40. Scale 9.7 - 8.4 = 17 lbs, half is 8½. The Moon is Significator, being only two degrees from the lower Meridian. It shows middle weight to win. Top weight won namely ELKINGTON.

Same day at 2.15, the Sun being on a cusp is Significator. On a scale of 8.4 - 6.6 or 26 lbs. It won by ROSCIUS.

On the 6th August at 1.40 the Moon was Significator being nearest to a cusp and its measure was 28/62. It was supported by the Sun. It won by PURO 7.9, nearest to indicated weight, but there was another at the same weight and the odds were too small to back both, so we pass it over, merely showing that the winner was indicated.

Same day at 2.15, the Sun was Significator and its distance was 34/56. It was supported by the Moon and Fortuna so far as the light weight was concerned and they all pointed to BLUE DANUBE who won.

NOTE

The Moon and Fortuna are not here pulling together but at a considerable angle, but near enough to indicate the same horse. In order to produce a reversal of the Measure of the Significator the other two factors must be the same or nearly the same distance from THE SAME ANGLE as one another, and though they agree together they must not agree with the Significator.

Example - August 15th at 2 pm where the Moon and Fortuna are pulling against the Sun which is Significator. The scale 9.0 - 7.6 gives 8.7 MY RONALD winner.

Thus it is seen that the Eclipse System justifies itself and the confidence of its discoverer.

THE SOLAR LUNAR VALUES

&

THE SOLAR APEX METHOD

BY

SEPHARIAL

The Solar Lunar Values by Sepharial

Rules:

Find the degree and sign held by the Sun/Moon at the previous and next Lunation.

Take the distance in degrees of longitude from the nearest Cardinal Point - also take the compliment of the Lunar distance from the cardinal point Aries, Cancer, Libra and Capricorn.

Generally one of these Lunations will be on a date previous to the race and the other an a date following the race.

They represent the "angular positions of joint Sun and Moon influences" in the circle.

Divide the runners by one quarter of the scale of weights. Let ¼, ½ and ¾ of the scale represent 0° Cancer; 0° Libra; 0° Capricorn. The top and bottom weights are represented by 0° Aries.

Multiply the Sun/Moon joint measures by ¼, ½, and ¾ of the scale and divide by 90.

Add to the top weight and deduct from the bottom weight.

For a check method of selecting from these weights, use the Nonal series as instructed in the Golden Key.

The Solar Apex Method by Sepharial

Draw the map as usual for the time of the race and place only the Sun's position.

Note the distance of the Sun from MC and Horizon Ascendant or Descendant.

Call that the 1st measure.

Take that number of degrees from 90 and call 2nd measure.

To the lesser of the two measures, add 45 and call this 3rd measure.

Multiply half the scale by those 3 measures and divide by 90: Deduct from the top weight and add to the bottom weight, giving six weights.

Take the BEST FORM horse of those six weights.

COSMOLOGICAL ECONOMICS

THE MASTERS OF FINANCIAL ASTROLOGY SERIES

The Masters of Financial Astrology Series brings together a collection of the most important classical and modern works on Astroeconomics or astrological financial market forecasting. These classic works written from the Golden Age of Technical Analysis to current times were carefully selected by the late Dr. Jerome Baumring of the Investment Centre Bookstore in the 1980's, as representing the most valuable and important works in financial astrology ever written. They were included as the foundational source texts for his program in advanced financial market analysis and forecasting, and serve as the ideal foundation for any analyst seeking a thorough education in astrological applications to financial market theory and forecasting.

The Golden Age of technical analysis was a period from the early 1900's through the 1960's where the foundational theories of modern financial analysis and financial astrology came into full form. The ideas and technologies developed during this fruitful period include the first serious research into the modern field of Astro-Economics, or Financial Astrology and related fields like cycle analysis, cosmic causation, solar influence on geomagnetic and Earthly events like weather, earthquakes, climate change and radio disturbance. Though financial astrology is actually a subject that stretches back centuries, if not millennia, this ripe period saw the real advent of popular research and theoretical development of this vast study of the interaction between cosmic forces and Earthly phenomena. This collection represents the best work available within this field.

Each quality reprint of these classical texts has been reproduced as an exact facsimile of the original text, maintaining the original layout, typeset, charts, and style of the author and time period, helping to preserve and communicate a sense of the feeling of the original work that a reproduction in modern format does not capture. Many of these rare works and courses were originally printed in only very small private editions or as correspondence courses, so that the originals were easily lost or destroyed over time. Our reproductions of these important source works are printed on acid free paper and bound in a quality hardcover that will compliment any trading library and help to preserve this important resource for generations to come.

The series is also currently being digitized and archived for permanent digital preservation by the Institute of Cosmological Economics, creating a searchable reference library of market wisdom accessible globally and available in new digital formats to keep the knowledge fresh and accessible through new devices and technology as we advance further into the information revolution. To see our full catalog of hardcover reprints, new publications, and digital editions please visit our website at www.CosmoEconomics.com.

- ❖ **Professor Weston** - Forecasting The New York Stock Market - *A Treatise on the Geometrical or Chart System of Forecasting* - (1921)
- ❖ **Louise McWhirter** - The McWhirter Theory Of Stock Market Forecasting - *The Theory & Application of Forecasting Trends & Cycles* - (1938)
- ❖ **James Mars Langham** - Planetary Effects On Stock Market Prices - *The Effects & Applications of Planetary Positions & Aspects on Prices* - (1932)
- ❖ **James Mars Langham** - Cyclical Market Forecasting Stocks & Grains - A Complete Course of Instruction in an Original & Proven System - (1938)

- **Fakir Chandra Dutt** - Market Forecasting - *A Scientific Exposition Of The Influences Of The Heavenly Bodies On The Fluctuations Of Values* - (1949)

- **Richard Scott** - The Planetary Market Barometer - *Trading Stocks, Futures & Forex With Celestial Mechanics* - (2015)

- **Fred White, Professor Weston, W. D. Gann, Sepharial** - The Earliest Financial Astrology Manuscripts - *The Original Works of The Old Masters* - (1902)

- **Donald Bradley** - Stock Market Prediction - *The Historical & Future Siderograph Charts & Software* - (1948)

- **Donald Bradley** - Collected Works of Donald Bradley - *Stock Market Prediction. Picking Winners. The Parallax Problem in Astrology. Solar & Lunar Returns. Profession & Birth Date. Taking the Kid Gloves off Astrology.* - (1950)

- **Sepharial (Walter Gorn Old)** - Sepharial's Arcana & Keys - *The Arcana of Stock & Share Key. Key to Sugar Values. Rubber. The Master Key. The Golden Key. The Eclipse System. The Solar Lunar Values. The Solar Apex Method.* - (1930)

- **J. Ross Tyler** - Financial Astrology - *The Key To Universal Law* - (1934)

- **Dr. Alexander Goulden** - Secrets of the Chronocrators - *An Advanced Course in Astrological Forecasting of Financial Markets* - (2014)

- **Dr. Alexander Goulden** - Behind the Veil - *Celestial Mechanics & Ancient Geometry in Financial Analysis* - (2010)

- **Daniele Prandelli** - The Law Of Cause And Effect - *Creating A Planetary Price/Time Map Of Market Action Through Sympathetic Resonance* - (2010)

- **T. G. Butaney, Financial Astrologer** - Forecasting Prices - *A Complete Course of Commercial Astrology* - (1940)

- **T. G. Butaney, Financial Astrologer** - How To Forecast Prices & Winners In Horse Races - *With Astrological Forecast Of Prices Or Cotton, Grains, Oil-Seeds & Rainfall* - (1947)

- **T. G. Butaney, Financial Astrologer** - Master Key Of Races - *All My Numerological & Astrological Secrets Discovered Over 30 Years' Experience* - (1970)

- **William D. Gann** - Collected Writings of W. D. Gann, Volume VI - *Astrological Writings* - (1955)

- **Muriel & Louis Hasbrouck** – Space Time Forecasting of Economic Trends – (1958-1006)

- **George Bayer** - Money Investing In Stocks, Trading In Commodities, Or The Time Factors In The Stock Market - *The Art of Scientifically Detecting Direction & Distance of Swings* - (1937)

- **George Bayer** - A Complete Course In Astrology - *Erection & Interpretation Of Horoscopes As Well As For Stocks* - (1937)

- **George Bayer** - Turning Four Hundred Years Of Astrology To Practical Use & Other Matters - (1944)

- **George Bayer** - Bible Interpretation - (1937)

- **Daniel T. Ferrera** - Studies In Astrological Bible Interpretation - (2001)

- **George J. McCormack** - Long-Range Astro-Weather Forecasting - *A Private, Comprehensive Technical Instruction Course* - (1965)

- **George J. McCormack** - ASTROTECH – *A Collection of Journals on Astrological Finance* - (1937-1941)

- **John Nelson** - Cosmic Patterns - (2006)

- **Thomas H. Graydon** - New Laws For Natural Phenomena - (1938)

- **W. T. Foster** - Sun Spots And Weather - (1907)

- **Cornelius Walford** - Famines Of The World - *Past & Present* - (1879)

- **Prof. Jos. Rodes Buchanan, M. D.** - Periodicity - *The Law Of All Life* - (1912)

- **Ray & Josephine Smythe** - Stars Ahead - (1942)

- **Sam Bartolet** - Eclipses & Lunations In Astrology - (1937)

- **Effie M. Cooley** - Astrological Relation Of Names & Numbers - (1912)

- **L. Edward Johndro** - Collected L. Edward Johndro - *The Stars, How And Where They Influence. The Earth in the Heavens. A New Concept of Sign Rulership. Astrological Dictionary & Self-Reading Horoscope* - (1927)

- **L. Edward Johndro** - Johndro's Collected Articles - 1930's - (1930)

- **Maurice Wemyss** - The Wheel Of Life Or Scientific Astrology - *5 Volumes Bound in 2 Hardcovers* - (1927)

- **Robert DeLuce** - Rectification Of The Horoscope - *Practical Lessons, Tables & Illustrations* - (1930)

- **Fred White** - A Guide To Astrology - *& Correcting The Time Of Birth* - (1901)

- **Gregorius** - The Master Key Of Destiny - (1924)
- **Paul Councel** - Your Stars And Destiny - (1940)
- **Mark Mellen** - How To Play The Races And Win - (1938)